"In the far-famed valley of the Merrimack rests our imperial city. Her streets, in regular and far-extended lines, are embowered by the sheltering elm and maple; her squares and parks lie like emeralds upon her bosom, while far and wide her broad expanse is studded with her imposing public buildings, her stately business blocks, her magnificent residences and her gigantic mills and shops."

— *Henry E. Burnham, 1927*

The Torrent No. 5 and members of the Manchester Veteran Fireman's Association, 1905. Photographer unknown

Picturing Manchester

A Selection of Images from the Manchester Historic Association

**Photographs from the
Manchester Historic Association Collection**

*Text by Betty Lessard
Edited by Holly Babin*

Machester Historic Association • Manchester, New Hampshire

Additional copies are available from the Manchester Historic Assocation, 129 Amherst Street, Manchester, NH 03101.
Printed in the United States of America.
Design by Nikki Bonenfant
Cover Photograph: The Notre Dame Bridge, 1983. Photo by Ernest Gould
ISBN: 0-9660881-0-7

Foreword

*from the Director
of the Manchester Historic Association*

The Manchester Historic Association was founded in 1896 on the occasion of the semi-centennial anniversary of the founding of the city of Manchester. For over one hundred years staff, volunteers, trustees, members, and area residents have worked together to make the Association a rich and vital historical resource for the community. These efforts are represented in the many educational programs and exhibits that have been presented by the MHA, and in our collections.

The collections of the Historic Association include a diverse range of materials that document the accomplishments of many people who have lived and worked in Manchester. Stone tools from Native American sites, the personal belongings of General John Stark, industrial artifacts from the Amoskeag Manufacturing Company together provide a tangible link to events in the city's past.

One of the most important and frequently used components of the collections are historical photographs. Thousands of cased photographs, cabinet cards, albums, prints and negatives make up a spectacular collection which provide a visual record of the changing nature of city life.

The care and development of these materials has been guided by Betty Lessard for nearly 30 years. This project was organized in honor of her dedication to the Association, and in celebration of our one hundredth anniversary in 1996.

Picturing Manchester is intended as a visual scrapbook of city memories. It has been organized to showcase a small portion of the Association's collections and to convey a sense of the city's distinctive past.

John Mayer, *Director*
Manchester Historic Association

Introduction

from the Historian
of the Manchester Historic Association

Photographs are wonderful visual documents. They bring immediacy, convey information, and provide a visual record to the viewer. Photographs preserve actions, evoke memories, and stimulate thought.

I selected the photographs for this book from the collections of the Manchester Historic Association. The images represent my interests and memories of the city's history, and I have assembled them to share my thoughts about Manchester.

My interest in the history of Manchester was unavoidable. My father told me tales of his growing up in the city — how he interacted with a circle of relatives and with friends in businesses and professions; of his opportunities to participate in civic events and celebrations; and of his wonder watching the city grow through a wide range of construction projects.

Early on, we made regular visits to the Historic Association. The displays were carefully explained, eclectic, and in place for extended periods. I was infected with the spirit of local pride that those exhibits communicated.

I came to the Historic Assocation in November of 1969, at the behest of David Goodwin, a Trustee and began my work with the library collections. I had been working at the Bedford Public Library when David asked me to fill-in while the Director, Virginia Plisko, was on maternity leave. So began for me this long, interesting, and delightful career.

I would like to acknowledge the patrons of the Manchester Historic Association whose interest in Manchester's history led them to donate some marvelous pictures of places and events.

John Mayer, director of the MHA, conceived of this project and guided the formation of the book. The MHA staff loyally encouraged the process, particularly Kevin Shupe and Peggy Hodges. Holly Babin and our friends at Business NH Magazine put it all in final form.

A very special thanks to my son, Charles E. Lessard, Jr., who with patience and restraint guided my work on the project. He helped me in the use of computers, provided the equipment and the manuals, and spent hours working with me — on the phone at dinner time, as well as during Sunday visits over coffee and donuts. No amount of thanks is enough.

Betty Lessard, *Historian*
Manchester Historic Association

The Locomotive "Henry Hobbs," circa 1865

Hollis and Canal streets
Photographer unknown

An engineer proudly displays the "Henry Hobbs" locomotive and its wood carrying tender in front of Manchester Locomotive Works.

The engine's lavish art decorations include a portrait of Henry Hobbs. While we know nothing about Hobbs, it was customary to name locomotives for principal investors in the railroad line. The design techniques used were a carry-over from stage coach artwork.

The Manchester Locomotive Works engine shed still stands on Canal Street at the foot of Hollis Street.

Manchester House, circa 1866

Merrimack Common, Elm and Merrimack streets
A. W. Kimball, photographer

Manchester House, the area's first hotel, was built in 1839, seven years before Manchester became a city. The hotel was distinguished from the stagecoach inns on the outskirts of town by virtue of its location near Manchester's manufacturing area.

Often, men with commercial interest in the city's new textile mills conducted business at the hotel. Stark Mill announced its first stock dividend at a dinner held there in 1839. Locals referred to the hotel as "Shepherd's Tavern" because William Shepherd and his wife managed the business for many years.

Manchester House stood at the corner of Elm and Merrimack streets until 1894. Merrimack Common is now Veterans Park.

Aretas Blood House, circa 1875

154 Lowell Street
Photographer unknown

Aretas Blood, head of Manchester Locomotive Works, lived in this home at the corner of Lowell and Union streets during the late 1800s. Lowell Street was a fashionable address and the house reflected the success of the locomotive manufacturer.

The house was torn down in 1963, but some of its iron work was preserved by a local resident.

Ash Street School, 1876
Bridge and Ash streets
Photographer unknown

Erected in 1873, the Ash Street School won national and international recognition for its elegant and progressive design. George W. Stevens, an engineer with Amoskeag Manufacturing Company, designed the building at the request of School Superintendent William Buck.

Stevens' design features a clover-leaf shape and tall, wide sash windows that allow each classroom to receive daylight from three sides. The school also boasts intricate brick work, granite trim, a Mansard third floor and rich wood details. Students could exit the building on the ground floor quickly through four entrances. Two broad stairways allowed children to exit from four classrooms on the second floor. Manchester officials sent a model of the school to the Centennial Exhibition of 1876 and the city received a medal for the school's innovative design. The emperor of Brazil requested the right to build a school like it in his country.

School children filled the hallways for 100 years. The school now serves as administrative headquarters for the Manchester School District. The Ash Street School was placed on the National Register of Historic Places in 1975.

John B. Clarke Family and Staff, 1876

146 Lowell Street
Photographer unknown

At the time of this photograph, Lowell Street was one of the most fashionable streets in the city. Shown are John B. Clarke's household staff, providing some fresh air for the family's pets and escorting the women of the household in a barouche pulled by a pair of matched carriage horses. The household staff probably included a footman, an upstairs maid, a parlor maid and a cook.

John B. Clarke published *The Manchester Daily Mirror*, a prominent local newspaper. Clarke loved horses and raised Standardbreds for sulky racing on the Mirror Farm at the south end of Elm Street.

The Clarke house stood until 1954, when it was demolished to make room for the Hartnett Parking lot.

Manchester Locomotive Works, circa 1880
Looking southwest from Dow Street
Seaver, Photographer

In 1854, Aretas Blood and Oliver Bayley of Vulcan Works bought patents for locomotive production from Amoskeag Manufacturing Company. They chartered their new company as Manchester Locomotive Works. Soon, the manufacturer was producing 14 locomotives a month.

In 1872, Manchester Locomotive Works bought rights from Amoskeag to produce self-propelled steam fire engines. These revolutionary engines were made until the gasoline engine became the standard in the early 20th century.

A Dressmaker and her Staff, circa 1880

Photographer's Studio
J. G. Ellinwood, photographer

Dressmakers, sometimes advertising themselves as tailoresses, were the female entrepreneurs of the 1800s. Many had several seamstresses on staff and ran a lucrative trade.

As more women entered the work force, the demand for business dresses grew. The elaborate fashions of the day required skilled needlework. Gussets, ruffles, shirring and fagoting decorated the bodices and skirts of dresses. Talented seamstresses found dressmaking an alternative to work in the mills.

Employees in Amoskeag Millyard, circa 1880

Bedford Street, below Stark Street
Photographer unknown

These Amoskeag Manufacturing Company employees may have gathered to welcome President Hayes who visited Manchester in 1880 as a guest of former New Hampshire governor Frederick Smyth.

The photo is taken on Bedford Street, behind the counting house and canal buildings and in front of what is now Tower Mill.

Manchester City Hall, circa 1885

Market and Elm streets
J. G. Ellinwood, photographer

Manchester's City Hall was designed by architect Edward Shaw of Boston and built in 1845. Amoskeag Manufacturing Company donated the lot on Elm Street and urged residents to move the town government from its home on Mammoth Road to a spot closer to the Millyard. Residents of the more populated millyard easily voted in the change of location at the town meeting of 1841.

As construction began, the building was known as the Town House. It became City Hall on September 8, 1846, when the city was chartered. In 1896, the main entryway was moved from Market Street to Elm Street and the city evicted retailers occupying the ground level. In 1976 the clock tower and spires were restored and a new Howard clock installed to commemorate the nation's bicentennial. Manchester City Hall is listed on the National Register of Historic Places. Plans are underway to move the entrance to its original position on Market Street.

Opera House Block, 1885

Hanover Street, between Elm and Chestnut streets
Photographer unknown

Opera patrons entered the four-story Opera House Block through the elegant two-story archway at the center of the building's facade. Retail businesses occupied many of the block's street level and second floor bays, while professional offices and apartments were in the upper stories. The block was also known as the Harrington-Smith Block, in reference to two of its principal investors. Adjoining the Opera House Block on the right was the Mirror Block, home to *The Manchester Daily Mirror* newspaper from 1854 to 1922.

In later years, the Opera House became a movie theatre. In 1979, fire ripped through the alley end of the building. Developers demolished the theatre when they renovated the fire damaged structure.

The Kennard, circa 1890

Elm Street looking west at Water Street
J. G. Ellinwood, photographer

Built in 1886, the six-story steel and granite Kennard Building was the pride of Manchester. It was the tallest building in the city and the first steel-framed structure in the area. Posh retailers occupied the ground level, and highly respected professional tenants worked in offices on the upper floors.

The building was a testament to the modern conveniences of the day with central heating, electricity, elevators and two washrooms on each floor. Tenants enjoyed the view from large windows and spacious rooms.

The interior was finished in fine woods. The roof boasted a sky-walk.

Although the Kennard was considered fireproof, the building succumbed to fire in January of 1902. The quality structure contained the intense heat, causing the steel to buckle and the building to collapse. Investors, mainly the Kennard family, built a smaller four-story building on the site. Developers tore down the smaller building in 1969 to make way for Hampshire Plaza.

Harvey District School, 1890

South Willow Street and Huse Road
Photographer unknown

Jonas Harvey, a prosperous owner of mills on Cohas Brook, built this brick schoolhouse in 1865. It served a school district for the southeast part of the city formed in 1791.

The two doorways segregated boys and girls when they entered and left the four-room schoolhouse. Once inside, the children sat together in class. The small school was renovated and expanded several times over the years, and was still in use in the 1950s.

A group of Manchester residents tried to save the school, but developers demolished the Victorian building in 1995 to make room for the Mall of New Hampshire expansion.

St. Joseph Cathedral, 1893

Pine and Lowell streets
Photographer unknown

Parishioners helped build St. Joseph Cathedral in 1865. This building was the second Roman Catholic church in the city and was built to accommodate a growing population of Irish immigrants. Architect Richard Keeley of Brooklyn, New York designed the cathedral, and contractor Alpheus Gay of Manchester built it. Gay had help from parishioners who reported directly to the construction site after a day of work at the mills.

In 1886, the Roman Catholic Church formed the Diocese of Manchester, and Dennis Bradley was named Bishop. The Bishop resided in the square brick building at the back of the church. In 1986, the church celebrated the diocese's 100th birthday with processions and special masses.

St. Augustin's Roman Catholic Church, 1893

Beech and Auburn streets
J. G. Ellinwood, photographer

St. Augustin's Church was built to meet the needs of a growing population of French-Canadian Catholics. The church was designed by architect George W. Dickey and built by Mead and Mason Contractors of Concord. The church was dedicated in 1873.

Amoskeag Manufacturing Company recruiting efforts brought many French speaking Canadians to Manchester. In response to requests for a French liturgy, a young French-Canadian priest, Reverend Augustin Chevalier, moved from northern New York to Manchester in 1870. Chevalier, the city's first Franco-American priest, immediately began to build the church and established a parish school.

The church bell was blessed in December 1884 and it announced services for the first time on New Year's Day 1885. The parish flourished and supported many other institutions, including the school, the St. Vincent de Paul orphanage and St. Cecilia Hall. The school has been converted to housing for the elderly.

The Unitarian Church, 1893

Beech and Concord streets
Photographer unknown

The Unitarian Church, on the corner of Beech and Concord streets, was designed by local architect George W. Dickey and built in 1872. Ornate stained glass windows and a row of American Elm trees along Beech Street enhanced the English Decorated style of the building.

Dickey also designed St. Augustin's Roman Catholic church in Manchester. The architect mysteriously disappeared in Boston in 1872.

By the middle of the 20th century, the Unitarian Church congregation could no longer support the costly maintenance of the large church and joined with the smaller Universalist Church. The building was razed in 1964.

E.A. Straw Mansion, 1893

Elm Street, between Harrison and Brook streets
James Woods, photographer

Ezekiel A. Straw built this imposing home on Elm Street when he was governor of New Hampshire in 1865. In 1838, at the age of 18, Straw came to Manchester as an engineer of Amoskeag Manufacturing Company. Working under the direction of William Amory, Amoskeag's Boston-based treasurer, Straw laid out Manchester's streets in a grid pattern and placed mills and accompanying housing along the river.

Straw was popular with both his employers and the hundreds he employed as agent of Amoskeag Manufacturing Company.

His home property was later divided into several lots. The Masonic Temple, the Straw School and the Christian Science Church are on the property around his home today, and the mansion is now apartments.

The Dye House, 1895

South Main Street at the bridge over the Piscataquog River
Photographer unknown

This area along South Main Street was a busy industrial center. In colonial times, it was a transshipment point for great pines that were floated down the Piscataquog River from New Boston, Weare and Bradford. In the 19th century, thriving businesses in the area included chandlery shops for rivermen's supplies, a sawmill, a bobbin factory that supplied Amoskeag Manufacturing Company, and a dye house. Log Street is the only reminder of this rich history.

Barr and Clapp Building, circa 1895
Granite Square
A. H. Sanborn, photographer

The Barr and Clapp building was an active commercial center in Granite Square on Manchester's West Side. Constructed in 1865, the building was home to many small businesses, including a famous market and bakery. In 1922, fire damaged the building and destroyed its mansard roof and central tower. After the fire, businesses continued to serve customers from the street level.

The remnants of the historic building were demolished when developers rebuilt Granite Square in 1979.

Boston & Maine Railroad Station, circa 1895

Railroad Square, south of Granite Street
J. G. Ellinwood, photographer

Boston and Maine built this elaborate station in 1897, when it consolidated the Concord Railroad and the Manchester and Lawrence Railroad. The station was designed in the Richardsonian style by Boston and Maine's architects.

The rail yard distributed goods throughout the entire southern and central portion of the state. Presidents Theodore Roosevelt and William Howard Taft spoke from Railroad Square. Throughout the 20th century, as the interstate highway system grew, railroads lost business to the trucking industry.

In 1961, under chairman Patrick McGinnis, Boston and Maine demolished the building. Manchester Mayor John Mongan protested, but he was reminded that the station was Boston and Maine property.

Gould House, circa 1900

2321 Elm Street
Photographer unknown

Prominent local banker Henry Chandler built this home in 1897 for his daughter Mary and son-in-law Lewis Gould. The elaborate home, a copy of a French chateau, was given to the couple as a wedding gift.

Manchester's social elite rubbed elbows at fabulous parties in the residence in the early 1900s. Notre Dame College purchased the building in 1953. The house is now home to the administrative offices of the college.

Granite St. Bridge, circa 1900

Granite Street at the Merrimack River
J. G. Ellinwood, photographer

The ornate Granite St. Bridge featured trolley tracks down its center. Wagons traveled in opposite directions on either side of the trolley tracks. Builders installed railings to keep horses from bolting off the bridge when mill whistles blew.

The lacy steel-truss and latticework bridge replaced an earlier structure that was washed out by the flood of 1896. This bridge withstood the flood of 1936, but was eventually replaced in 1979.

Hallsville Grocery Co., 1900

Massabesic and Cypress streets
A. H. Sanborn, photographer

The Hallsville Grocery Co. was a popular stop along the railroad line from Manchester to Raymond. Commuters from Auburn, Candia and Raymond rode the line to their jobs in Manchester. Farmers used the stop to send produce, eggs and chickens to Manchester markets.

The railroad was operated by the Manchester and Lawrence Railroad. It provided an important service for the several shoe factories in East Manchester, Forsaith Machine Shop, the Elliot Silk Mills, Profile Bedding and Dunbar Coal Company — all vital industries in the area.

Kimball Brothers Shoe Factory, 1900

Massabesic and Cypress streets
Photographer unknown

In 1886, after moving from Raymond, New Hampshire, the Kimball brothers constructed this building to house their shoe factory. At the time, steam power allowed manufacturers to build plants away from water power sites along the Merrimack River. The Kimball brothers began a process of industrialization in a previously undeveloped area.

The building has been used by various manufacturers over the years. It is an apartment complex today.

Shirley Hill House, 1900
Goffstown
Photographer unknown

The Shirley Hill House is an example of a former farm turned resort. In the early 20th century, city residents retreated to the open spaces offered by these "summer hotels."

The resorts offered recreational activities such as tennis, hiking and billiards. Guests also made new acquaintances while relaxing on the porch or socializing at dances. A marked grass tennis court is evident in the foreground of this picture.

Manchester Kindergarten Association, 1902

Spring Street, between Elm and Canal streets
F. Frisselle, photographer

Manchester had its own public kindergarten in 1902, long before public kindergarten became the norm. Miss Parker, with the support of the Manchester Kindergarten Association, founded the school as a private venture in 1901. Although it opened the following year as a public kindergarten, the city school system didn't take over its operation for several years. By 1920, all Manchester schools offered public kindergarten.

Mrs. Sanborn and Mrs. Caswell, 1906

Photographer unknown

Mrs. A.H. Sanborn and Mrs. Fred Caswell enjoy a ride in a horseless carriage. This vehicle may have been produced by one of several local mechanics who built automobiles. In the early 20th century, Peter Harris, the Aalding Shop and the Johnstons all built horseless carriages in Manchester. This vehicle was powered either by steam or electricity.

Steam Fire Engine No. 1, 1910

Vine Street, between Amherst and Concord streets
Photographer unknown

Manchester Locomotive Works built the steam fire engine and wagon pictured here. Manchester's fire brigade poses in front of the Central Fire Station on the west side of Concord Square, now the Victory Parking Garage. Built in 1846, the station featured a wide yard that allowed dashing horses and equipment to make the turn in their haste to reach a fire.

Manchester Fire Dept. Engine No. 1 was elaborately detailed with red paint and brass fittings. The oncoming rush of equipment, the rumble of horses' hooves and the clanging of gongs and bells alerted city residents to a fire.

The Central Fire Station stood until 1972, when the new station was erected on Merrimack Street. The site is now occupied by a telephone company building.

Amoskeag Manufacturing Company Employee Housing, circa 1910

Market Street and Hampshire Lane
A. H. Sanborn, photographer

Amoskeag Manufacturing Company built this structure and others like it to house its management staff and their families. The company established an hierarchical housing system in which operatives lived in boarding rooms close to the mills, while managers lived close to Elm Street. This commodious double house features black bands beneath the windows on the first and second floors. Legend has it that the bands were placed there to mourn President Lincoln's assassination.

The house still stands at the corner of Market Street and Hampshire Lane.

St. Anselm Abbey and College, 1910

Shirley Hill Road, Goffstown
Photographer unknown

Benedictine monks built St. Anselm Abbey as a center to provide spiritual guidance. The monks came to the area to support the many Bavarian Roman Catholics who found work in the mills and settled on the West Side of Manchester.

The original structure, built in 1888, burned in 1897. The monks quickly replaced the building with this stately establishment. The college has attracted and educated generations of students. This building now houses the administrative offices of the college. Modern classrooms, dormitories and libraries sprawl across the growing campus. St. Anselm College is considered one of the best small liberal arts colleges in the country.

Charles H. Manning House, 1912

1838 Elm Street
Photographer unknown

Amoskeag Manufacturing Company built this home in 1894 for Charles H. Manning, an engineer, inventor and superintendent of the Amoskeag Steam Power Plant. The residence is one of many fine examples of Victorian architecture in the city.

The house still stands at 1838 Elm Street and is used as a place of business. Many other homes on the north end of Elm Street have been converted to business offices.

Homestead, Old Manchester Center, 1912

Mammoth Road
Photographer unknown

Prosperous local farmers, craftsmen and merchants built houses like this one in the 18th century. Long before textile mills drew the population toward the banks of the Merrimack, Mammoth Road was the center of community activity. A village of commerce and agriculture sprouted along the route. Local businesses produced lumber, flax, linen and potatoes. In 1751, with 30 families inhabiting the area, the community known as Derryfield was granted township status.

P.H. Dow House, 1912

55 North River Road
Photographer unknown

Motorists depart from the P.H. Dow House for an afternoon spin. Dow was the superintendent of the Land and Water Power Division of Amoskeag Manufacturing Company from 1891 until 1925.

Early motorists left prepared for disaster on the rough roads of the early 1900s. In case of a flat or two, these travelers have tied several spare tires to the running boards.

The house was demolished in the 1970's to build the Hampshire Towers apartments.

Amoskeag Baseball Team, 1913

Textile Field, Valley and Maple streets
Photographer unknown

The popularity of baseball caught on at area mills and several factories sponsored local teams. The teams, including the Amoskeag and Stark Mill teams, were members of the Manufacturer's League. They joined forces to play the Boston Red Sox on opening day of Textile Field, September 8, 1913.

Opening Day, Textile Field, 1913

Valley and Maple streets
Photographer unknown

Amoskeag Manufacturing Company built this stadium in 1913. Factory workers and loyal Manchester residents packed the stands for opening day celebrations, which featured a face off between the Boston Red Sox and all-stars from the Manufacturer's League. The Manufacturer's League featured teams whose players were workers in local factories, such as McElwain Shoe, Stark Manufacturing Company and Amoskeag Manufacturing Company. The Red Sox won the game 3 to 1.

The stadium, now known as Gill Stadium, still attracts a crowd.

Mount Uncanoonuc Hotel, 1914

Uncanoonuc Mountain, Goffstown
Photographer unknown

Visitors to the Mount Uncanoonuc Hotel braved a precarious ride on the Incline Railroad and hiked the last leg of the journey. Once there, they enjoyed spectacular views from the hotel's expansive porches and observatory.

Swimming Pavilion, 1915

Pine Island Park, Goffe's Falls
A. H. Sanborn, photographer

The swimming pavilion at Pine Island Park was a popular spot to pass a summer day. The site featured bath houses, life guard instructors and a fenced area for safety.

In the early 1900s, co-ed swimming was prohibited. Girls and boys had separate swimming periods. In this photo, girls in sashes and ribboned straw hats watch the boys swim as they await their turn in the water.

The Carousel, 1915

Pine Island Park, Goffe's Falls
Photographer unknown

The magnificent carousel at Pine Island Park was a favorite with children, parents and grandparents alike. The carousel was made by the Philadelphia Toboggan Company.

Pine Island was owned by the Manchester Traction, Light and Power Company, which later became Public Service Company of New Hampshire. Traction companies provided trolley transportation, the means of getting to suburban Goffe's Falls. Visitors to Pine Island enjoyed dancing, swimming, canoeing, roller skating, refreshments, a roller coaster and the carousel.

The carousel was destroyed by fire in 1961. Two years later, the park closed forever.

The Freight Yards and Boston & Maine Repair Shops, 1915

Elm Street, south of Granite Street
Photographer unknown

The Freight Yards served as a distribution point for most goods entering and leaving the state. Railway express clerks were kept busy routing wares from all over the nation in and out of the yard. Train crews shunted the great steam locomotives into the semi-round house for maintenance and repairs. This was an era of great prosperity for Manchester. Textiles, shoes and machined products were exported in quantity.

The Ragged Mountain Club, 1915

Ragged Mountain
Photographer unknown

Members of the Ragged Mountain Club relax after a long trek up the mountain. As disposable income grew, clubs like this sprouted up around the Queen City. Residents with similar interests would band together at clubs for boating, fishing and hunting. Membership and use of the clubs' facilities were strictly regulated.

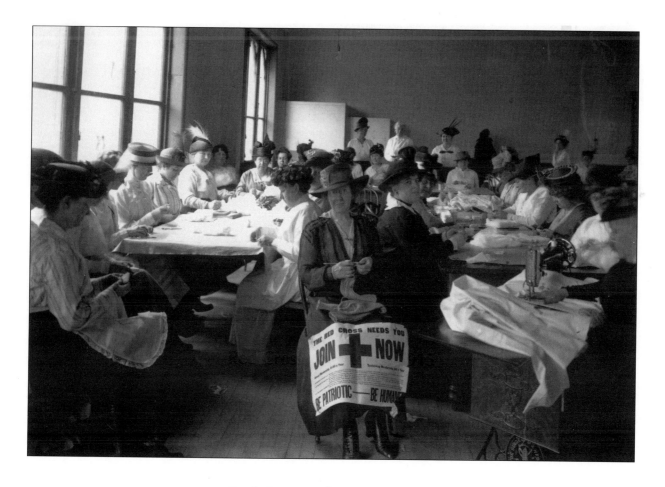

Red Cross Volunteers, 1915

City Hall
Photographer unknown

Before the United States formally entered World War I, women volunteers gathered at City Hall to produce supplies for England, France and Belgium. The women made linen compresses, rolled bandages, sheets, shirts, knitted socks, mittens, helmet liners and children's clothing. The Red Cross shipped the items to England and France for distribution.

Many of the women pictured served the Red Cross again during World War II. The elderly volunteers were known as the "Grey Ladies."

One Day's Product, 1915
Amoskeag Manufacturing Company
Photographer unknown

Amoskeag Manufacturing Company laborers produced this collection of fabrics in one day.

The Manchester textile company was famous for its "Amoskeag Fancy Cloths." Ginghams, intricate plaids, checks and stripes woven of dyed threads are shown in the foreground. Solid color heavier denims are shown toward the center of the photo. In the background are prints,

jacquards and mateleses. Swags of chambrays, lawns and dimities decorate the ceiling.

Those interested in the history of these fabrics are able to study sample books from Amoskeag Manufacturing Company in the collections of the Manchester Historic Association.

Amoskeag Covered Bridge, 1917
Amoskeag Falls on the Merrimack River
Photographer unknown

The Amoskeag bridge was built in 1854 by a group of private investors. The bridge provided a crossing at the falls until it collapsed on a September night in 1920. The structure had rotted from many years of service.

Amoskeag is a Penacook word meaning "place of many fish."

Native people fished at the falls for thousands of years prior to European settlement.

Amoskeag Manufacturing Company built the dam just north of the bridge to store the river's energy, equivalent to about 15,000 horsepower.

Manchester Brownie Swim Team, circa 1920

Amoskeag Ledge Quarry
Photographer unknown

The Manchester Brownies chopped through ice at the Amoskeag Ledge quarry and leapt into the frigid water on winter Sunday afternoons. The group provided entertainment for curious residents who lined the ledges around the quarry pool to watch their antics. The Brownies also drew the attention of a newsreel company, which documented their adventures.

Kindergarten, 1920

North Street, between Elm Street and River Road
Photographer unknown

This private kindergarten served children from wealthy families in Manchester.
These 6-year-olds learned according to the Montessori method of teaching.

Amoskeag Bank Building, Barton's Store and Merchant's Bank Building, 1920

Elm and Manchester streets
Photographer unknown

In 1914, the Amoskeag Bank built the white 10-story limestone building at the left of the photograph. At the time, it was the tallest building in Manchester. Several months after it opened, a fire in the Merchants Exchange next door displaced several businesses and sullied the new bank exterior with soot.

One of the displaced businesses, Barton's, rebuilt the elegant five-story ladies department store shown in this photograph. In 1919, the Merchants Bank added the marble edifice in the foreground as an anchor to this block of early 20th century businesses.

Amoskeag Bank demolished Barton's (then known as Leavitt's) and Merchants Bank in 1979 to make room for its new offices. Citizens Bank of New Hampshire now occupies the site.

Trolley Car Barns, circa 1920

Traction Street
Photographer unknown

Trolley cars, shown here in their Traction Street barns, carried residents throughout the Queen City from the early 1900s to the 1940s, when motor buses came on the scene. The Manchester Power, Light and Traction Company (renamed Public Service Company in 1929) operated the electric trolleys.

Open cars were used during the summer and closed cars during winter. An overhead wire system carried energy to power the trolleys. Maintenance cars and snow plows kept the vehicles on line.

Traction Street disappeared when the Center of New Hampshire was developed in the 1970s.

Hanover Street, 1920

Looking west from Chestnut Street
Photographer unknown

Manchester residents nicknamed Hanover Street "the great white way" after New York City's famous theatre district. The street boasted 22 theatres between Chestnut and Elm streets and and was lined with bright white street lights.

Residents could view traditional theatre at the Opera House, vaudeville shows at the Palace Theatre or movies at the Crown Theatre.

Visitors to performances at auditoriums in the Odd Fellows Block and meetings at church and volunteer halls also kept the area busy throughout the evening.

A small corner park now occupies the site of the florist shop on the left.

Reverend A. S. Yantis House, circa 1921

266 Harrison Street
Photographer unknown

This Harrison Street residence is typical of many early 20th century homes in middle class Manchester neighborhoods. Reverend A. S. Yantis lived here with his wife and children. Reverend Yantis served as the pastor of the Unitarian Church from 1917 to 1922.

Notice the large porch on the front of the house. Neighbors interacted and shared news of their community from porches like this. When Amoskeag Manufacturing Company went bankrupt in the spring of 1936, a committee of local residents walked the neighborhoods, selling shares of the newly formed Amoskeag Industries to people relaxing on their porches.

Shell Oil Station, circa 1922

South Main and Parker streets
Photographer unknown

The owners of this Victorian mansion paid their tax bill by leasing space to a Shell Oil Station. The 1860s mansion was the former home of the Parker family.

Francis Wayland Parker grew up in the home. He later founded the teacher's college that became Chicago University. Children still compete in a New Hampshire essay contest bearing Parker's name.

The mansion was a showpiece well into the 1930s. Today, a block of retail stores occupies the site.

Baldwin Cafeteria, 1922

972 Elm Street
Photographer unknown

In 1922, the proprietor of Baldwin's allowed his downtown eatery to become part of the Waldorf's chain. Waldorf's was one of the first cafeteria-style eateries. Located in the heart of the Manchester business district, the shop allowed executives to break for a quick lunch. It was a welcome alternative to a trip home or a longer lunch spent at one of the area's private clubs. In 1923, the change was official — a Waldorf sign replaced the Baldwin logo.

Amoskeag Strike, 1922
Canal Street near Stark Street
Photographer unknown

A small group of workers march in protest against pay cuts and an increase in hours at Amoskeag Manufacturing Company. The company-wide strike drew national attention and Samuel Gompers, the renowned labor leader, visited Manchester to encourage the striking workers.

The strike continued for nine months, but the workers gained nothing.

They returned to work for longer hours and less pay. Amoskeag lost some of its best customers and middle managers during the strike. The factory, which once employed 17,000, produced fabrics on a diminishing scale until 1935.

First Motorized Paddy Wagon, 1923

Manchester and Chestnut streets
Photo by Lindsay Studio

Manchester's Police Department received its first motorized paddy wagon as part of Mayor George E. Trudel's program to improve the city's infrastructure. The new vehicle is shown in front of the Police Station that was built in 1882. It was torn down in 1978 to make way for the police station that stands today.

Ladder Co. No. 8, 1923

527 South Main Street
Edward A. Belisle, photographer

Mayor George E. Trudel's efforts to improve the city infrastructure resulted in a new hook and ladder for the South Main Street Fire Station. In addition to buying new equipment, Trudel's program benefited city residents through the construction of schools, highways, streets and fire and police stations. Trudel served as mayor from 1922 to 1925.

The Amoskeag Manufacturing Company Float, 1924

Winter Carnival Parade
Canal Street
Photographer unknown

Employees of Amoskeag Manufacturing Company and their children show off the company float as it readies for Manchester's annual Winter Carnival Parade. Each year, retailers and manufacturers tried to outdo each other with their entries. Snowshoe clubs including the Alpine, Davignon, Richelieu and several from Canada marched in the parade, too.

Ice skating, dog sled races, tobogganing, skiing and the antics of the Manchester Brownies Swimming Club were all part of the week long Winter Carnival.

Chase Family Homes, 1924

Shasta Street
Photographer unknown

This home is one of many affordable homes built in Manchester by Edward Chase. Chase was a Lithuanian immigrant and successful merchant who felt the public should be protected from landlords who refused to rent to families with children. He established the Chase Family Association fund, which made it possible to buy a home with no down payment. For a weekly payment of $7.50 over a 21 year period, working class families could own one of his homes.

Chase sited the houses on modest tracts of land on Montgomery, Hevey, Shasta and Maple streets and Cilley and Mammoth roads. Each home was designed with the same basic floor plan: three rooms upstairs with a bathroom; and a kitchen/pantry, dining room and living room on the first floor.

Checker Cab Company, 1924

Kosciuszko Street near Bridge Street
Photographer unknown

In 1924, the Checker Cab Company opened this new garage on Kosciuszko Street, formerly Birch Street.

Many families could either not afford their own car or didn't have space to build a garage in the dense neighborhoods of the city. Taxis were an alternative and people used cabs routinely.

The Checker Cab Company thrived until the mid-1930s, when the Depression hit. The building stands today on the renamed Kosciuszko Street. The checker design is still faintly visible.

Varick Advertising Sign, circa 1925

Location unknown
Photographer unknown

Billboards advertised goods and services to travelers on Manchester's early highways. The John B. Varick Co. was a huge agricultural and sporting goods department store that competed with Sears in the Manchester area.

Over the years, age and weather left unsightly billboards along highways. First Lady "Lady Bird" Johnson abolished dilapidated billboards with her highway beautification program in the 1960s.

St. Anthony Church and School, 1927

Belmont and Silver streets
Photographer unknown

In 1927, the St. Anthony School House was built to replace a simpler wooden parish building. Although St. Anthony's served French-speaking parishioners, both English and French were taught at the school.

Local sculptor Lucien Gosselin created gargoyles for the entry and plaques set into the walls of the new school. St. Anthony was one of five French-speaking parishes in the city. The others were Ste. Marie, St. Augustin's, St. John Baptiste and St. George.

World War I Memorial, 1928

Victory Park, Chestnut and Amherst streets
A. H. Sanborn, photographer

Lucien Gosselin, a local sculptor, designed this victory monument and sculpted its figures. The park, formerly known as Concord Common, was renamed Victory Park in honor of World War I veterans.

With Bishop Guertin's support, Gosselin studied art in Paris. Many of Gosselin's sculptures can be seen throughout the city, adorning schools, church grounds and cemeteries.

Opening Night, State Theatre, November 27, 1929

1114 Elm Street
Photographer unknown

State Theatre was considered one of the finest Art Deco buildings north of Boston. The theatre opened in 1929 with the latest in sound technology. Interior features included spacious lobbies, magnificent chandeliers and broad stairways. The building's facade boasted colored windows, mosaic patterns in the brick work and a mask of Comus created by Italian stone masons from Boston.

Three generations of moviegoers found entertainment at the State Theatre. It was demolished in 1978 to make way for the Wall Street Executive Center. St. Anselm College saved the mask of Comus. It can be seen opposite the Dana Center on the college campus.

The Planned City, 1930

Aerial view of downtown Manchester
Chester Davis, photographer

In 1838 William Amory, treasurer of the Boston-based Amoskeag Manufacturing Company, devised the planned grid of leafy squares, commercial streets and row housing captured in this aerial view of the city. Amory designed the city to support production of cotton textiles.

As the city prospered and expanded, residential neighborhoods with churches and schools developed toward Mammoth Road. Business people working in the downtown area still find the compact street layout easy to navigate.

Pariseau's Ladies Department Store, 1931

Elm Street, between Concord and Amherst streets
Photographer unknown

Despite the hard times of the Depression, T. Pariseau decorated his store and helped brighten Elm Street for the Christmas Season. Pariseau's opened as a shoe store in 1912. The business was soon established as a stylish women's fashion store and remained a favorite with customers well into the 1970s.

The structure housing Pariseau's was built in 1854 as the Music Hall. In the 1950s, its fancy brick work was replaced with flat, windowless white brick. In the 1980s, the entire facade was removed and a steel front was applied. The building is now known as the Atrium.

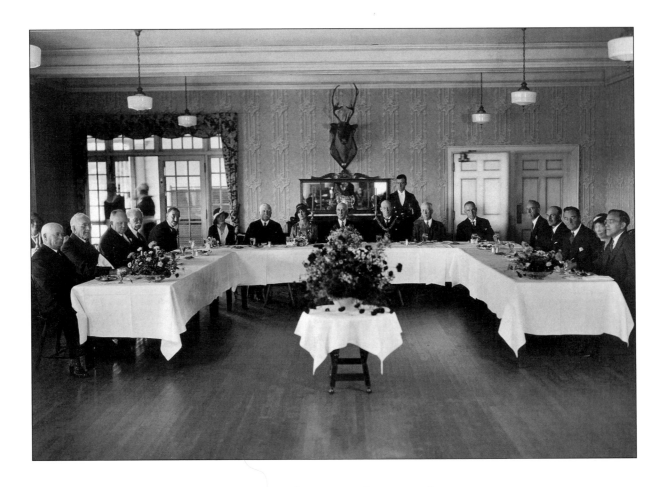

Banquet for the Lord Mayor Titt, October 10, 1931

Manchester Country Club, Bedford
Photographer unknown

Lord Mayor Titt and the Lady Mayoress of Manchester, England were the guests of honor at this banquet commemorating the city's name change from Derryfield to Manchester. The 700 residents of the agricultural village of Derryfield approved the name change in 1810 in honor of Samuel Blodget who predicted that "at Amoskeag Falls, a city could rise like unto Manchester in England."

Beer Wagon at Rice-Varick Hotel, 1933

32 Merrimack Street
Photographer unknown

The arrival of this Anheuser-Busch beer wagon at the Rice-Varick Hotel marked the end of Prohibition in Manchester. Local residents and hotel patrons gathered to watch the conclusion of the 13-year ban on the manufacture, sale and transportation of alcoholic liquors. Many of them celebrated Prohibition's repeal with dinner and drinks at the hotel that evening.

Girl Scout Troop, 1933

Location unknown
Photographer unknown

This Girl Scout Troop was sponsored by the First Congregational Church. Most churches in the city had both Girl and Boy Scout troops. Scouting allowed children from different public schools to meet.

Before cookie sales, scout troops held paper drives and served church suppers to raise money. Uniforms were purchased one piece at a time and worn only for scouting.

Mill Interior following the Flood, 1936

Amoskeag Manufacturing Company
Photographer unknown

Amoskeag Manufacturing Company had filed bankruptcy and was awaiting authorization for its reorganization plan when the flood of 1936 wiped out hope of a comeback. The company had bought modern machinery to replace obsolete textile operations, but the new equipment was destroyed by the March flood waters.

In June, the court allowed Amoskeag Industries Inc., a local corporation, to raise money to buy the physical assets of Amoskeag Manufacturing Company in Manchester. The millyard was a busy industrial center for the next 40 years, kept alive by a diversified group of companies that bought or leased space in the former mill buildings. The companies included Pandora Mills, Chicopee Mills, Marion Electronics, Habitat Soups and Myrna Shoe.

Flood Cleanup, 1936

Granite Street
Photographer unknown

Occupants of tenement housing in the Granite and Second street area struggle to clean up debris left by the overflowing banks of the Merrimack River. The first floor apartments, usually owner occupied and the most desirable in the building, were hardest hit by the flood.

Most of this dense neighborhood was demolished in 1978 to make room for the expansion and renovation of the Everett Turnpike, Granite Bridge and Granite Square.

St. Mary's Bank, 1940

Amory and Main streets
Eric Sanford, photographer

La Caisse Populaire Ste. Marie, now known as St. Mary's Bank, was established in 1909 at the urging of Monsignor Hevey, the founder of Ste. Marie parish. Hevey felt the financial organizations of Manchester were not serving his French-Canadian parishioners.

This marble bank was demolished and the modern St. Mary's Bank erected in 1972. St. Mary's Bank is the oldest credit union in the United States.

New Hampshire Swimming Champion Meet, 1947

Rock Rimmon Pool
Photographer unknown

Each year, swimmers from schools, YMCAs and community recreation departments competed in the statewide championships held at Rock Rimmon Pool. A large group of fans turned out to cheer the athletes at the August 18th event. A canoe at pool's edge was ready for use as a lifeboat, if needed.

Manchester Women's Club, 1955

Wentworth-by-the-Sea
Lou Koch, photographer

Members of the Manchester Women's Club enjoy a conference and luncheon at Wentworth-by-the-Sea in New Castle. The organization was founded in 1895 to "work for the betterment of the community."

The volunteer group provides work in social services. Over the years, the group has supported a number of organizations, including the VA hospital, Special Olympics, the Girl Scouts, women's shelters and special schooling.

Elm Street, 1956

Looking south from Merrimack Street
Eric Sanford, photographer

Retailers on Elm Street stayed open late into the evening during the holiday season. Evergreen garlands decorate the newly installed street lights. Parking meters were another recent addition to Elm Street, the retail center of the city since its founding.

This shot is taken south of Merrimack Street, opposite Merrimack Common (now known as Veterans Park).

Merry-Go-Round, circa 1961

Pine Island Park
Photographer unknown

In the 1960s, this Merry-Go-Round featuring Disney Cartoon characters replaced an earlier carousel that whisked riders around on more traditional carousel horses.

Pine Island Park offered several amusements during this period. In the summer, an outdoor movie screen showed cartoons for children in the early evening and movies for their parents as the night progressed. Parents dressed their children in night clothes so they could enjoy the late movies as little ones drifted off to sleep.

The owners closed the park in 1963 when it failed to pay its own way.

Triple-Decker, 1970

180 Spruce Street
Gerda Peterich, photographer

Many immigrants settled in multi-tenanted apartment houses, such as this 12-unit dwelling built in 1915. Often, several families shared living space and older, retired family members watched over school-age children while their parents worked. Immigrants arriving from the same country would band together in these miniature neighborhoods.

As housing needs increased toward the end of the 19th century, builders raised the roofs on houses to add living space.

Urban Renewal in the Millyard, 1971

Looking west from Hampshire Plaza
Ernest Gould, photographer

By 1969, the buildings and infrastructure of Manchester's millyard were deteriorating and held no attraction for modern industry. An area once dominated by a few large companies was now fractured by multiple tenants, owners and vacancies. The city addressed the problem with an ambitious urban renewal project. As shown in this photo, the two canals running through the area were filled and about half of the aging buildings demolished.

The 1969 urban renewal project was the city's second attempt to address changes in the millyard. In 1935, a century of prosperity for

Manchester abruptly ended when Amoskeag Manufacturing Company declared bankruptcy. Mayor Arthur E. Moreau formed a committee "to buy the physical assets of Amoskeag Manufacturing Company in Manchester." The U.S. bankruptcy court accepted the committee's proposal, and set the price at $3 million. Manchester bankers and business owners raised the money and incorporated Amoskeag Industries Inc. to handle the assets and bring a new, more diversified group of manufacturers to the city. The group successfully filled the buildings with new businesses and the area served as an industrial base for the region for another 30 years.

Octagon House, 1972

Hanover and Belmont streets
Ernest Gould, photographer

The Octagon House on Hanover Street is one of three in Manchester based on the 1840s design by Orson Fowler. This home, built in 1866, features an octagonal barn. The octagon shape was intended to create low cost, low maintenance housing for moderate income families, but this brick version, purchased by Henry Joy, is more elegant than the other two.

The other two octagon houses were built in the 1850s. One is on Beech Street and the other is on Mast Road.

Manchester Institute of Arts & Sciences, circa 1984
148 Concord Street
Ernest Gould, photographer

Mrs. Emma Blood French donated the handsome Manchester Institute of Arts and Sciences building to promote music, crafts and practical and natural sciences. The building was designed by Edward L. Tilton of Gotham and Tilton, a New York firm.

Emma French was the daughter of Aretas Blood, an agent who made his fortune through Manchester Locomotive Works. Her contribution allowed residents to take studio classes and enjoy concerts, exhibits, films and visiting lecturers. To this day, residents continue to enjoy the diversified offerings of the Institute, now known as the New Hampshire Institute of Art.

Temple Adath Yeshurin, 1984

Beech and Prospect streets
Ernest Gould, photographer

Temple Adath Yeshurin, designed by architect Percival Goodman of New York, featured an outside art wall designed by Harris and Ros Barron of Boston. The art wall depicts religious symbols, such as the five scrolls, the pillar of fire, and the seven-branched Menorah under sun and sky.

The temple was built in 1954 when the congregation moved from its original Central Street location to its site on Beech and Prospect streets. One side of the temple features a garden with a memorial to holocaust victims. Armand Zainer, a Manchester resident and concentration camp survivor, designed the memorial.

St. George Greek Orthodox Cathedral, 1984

650 Hanover Street
Ernest Gould, photographer

This magnificent Greek Cathedral was designed by architect Christopher Kantianis of Springfield, Massachusetts. Built in 1965, it replaced the earlier Saint George Church on Pine and Hayward streets.

Greek immigrants recruited by the textile and shoe industries settled primarily in Spruce Street and Chestnut Street neighborhoods. The proprietors of many successful Manchester businesses, including the Puritan Restaurant and Van Otis Chocolates, trace their ancestry to Greece.

Notre Dame Bridge and Arms Park, 1989

Arms Park
Ernest Gould, photographer

The graceful Notre Dame Bridge opened in 1938, restoring a link between the neighborhoods on the west and east sides of the Merrimack River. The bridge replaced the McGregor Bridge, which was severely damaged during the flood of 1936. The Notre Dame Bridge was known as the "singing bridge" because car tires made a humming noise as they crossed its grid deck.

In the forefront of the photograph is Arms Park, a public gathering area created during the city's 1969 urban renewal project. The park is named for the Arms Textile Mill, a company that produced wool coats during the 1940s. The mill ceased production shortly after World War II. The building was incinerated in a cement block shell because of contamination by anthrax. Concerts, fairs and exhibitions are held at the park today.

New Notre Dame Bridge, 1990

Arms Park
Ernest Gould, photographer

In the late 1980s, engineers discovered the suspension arch and piers supporting the Notre Dame Bridge were in need of repair and in dangerous condition. They recommended the bridge be torn down and replaced. Residents protested. Engineers conducted a second study. The city examined several alternatives to demolition, but finally decided to replace the arched structure with a wider two-span, four-lane bridge. The new bridge was built higher than its predecessor to ease the steep descent from the east bank of the Merrimack River to the west.

The original Notre Dame Bridge was demolished in 1989. The new span opened in 1990.

Index of Photographs

Amoskeag Bank Building, Barton's Store and
　Merchant's Bank Building, 1920 54
Amoskeag Baseball Team, 1913 42
Amoskeag Covered Bridge, 1917 51
Amoskeag Manufacturing Company
　Amoskeag Strike, 1922...............................60
　Company Float, 1924 63
　Employee Housing, circa 1910 37
Ash Street School, 1876 13
Baldwin Cafeteria, 1922 59
Barr and Clapp Building, circa 1895 27
Beer Wagon at Rice-Varick Hotel, 1933 73
Blood House, Aretas, circa 1875.....................12
Boston & Maine Railroad Station, circa 1895 ...28
Chase Family Homes, 1924 64
Checker Cab Company, 1924 65
Clarke, John B. Family and Staff, 1876 14
Dow House, P.H., 1912 41
A Dressmaker and her Staff, circa 1880...........16
The Dye House, 1895 26
Elm Street, 1956 80
Employees in Amoskeag Millyard, circa 1880....17
Flood Cleanup, 1936 76
The Freight Yards and Boston & Maine Repair Shops, 1915 47
Girl Scout Troop, 1933 74
Gould House, circa 1900 29
Granite St. Bridge, circa 1900 30
Hanover Street, 1920 56
Hallsville Grocery Co., 1900...........................31
Harvey District School, 1890 21
Homestead, Old Manchester Center, 1912 40
The Kennard, circa 1890.................................20
Kimball Brothers Shoe Factory, 1900 32
Kindergarten, 1920 53
Ladder Co. No. 8, 1923 62
The Locomotive "Henry Hobbs," circa 1865 10
Manchester Brownie Swim Team, circa 1920.....52
Manchester City Hall, circa 1885.....................18
Manchester House, circa 1866 11
Manchester Institute of Arts & Sciences, circa 1984 85
Manchester Kindergarten Association, 1902 34
Manchester Locomotive Works, circa 1880........15

Manchester's Women's Club, 1955 79
Manning House, Charles H., 1912....................39
Mill Interior following the Flood, 1936 75
Mount Uncanoonuc Hotel, 1914.......................44
New Hampshire Swimming Champion Meet, 1947.......78
New Notre Dame Bridge, 1990.........................89
Notre Dame Bridge and Arms Park, 1989 88
Octagon House, 1972 84
One Day's Product, 1915.................................50
Opera House Block, 1885 19
Paddy Wagon, First Motorized, 1923................61
Pariseau's Ladies Department Store, 1931 71
Pine Island
　The Carousel, 1915.....................................46
　Merry-Go-Round, circa 1961 81
　Swimming Pavilion, 1915 45
The Planned City, 1930...................................70
The Ragged Mountain Club, 1915 48
Red Cross Volunteers, 1915.............................49
St. Anselm Abbey and College, 1910 38
St. Anthony Church and School, 1927 67
St. Augustin's Roman Catholic Church, 1893 ...23
St. Joseph Cathedral, 1893.............................22
St. George Greek Orthodox Cathedral, 1984 87
St. Mary's Bank, 1940.....................................77
Mrs. Sanborn and Mrs. Caswell, 1906 35
Shell Oil Station, circa 1922...........................58
Shirley Hill House, 1900 33
State Theatre, Opening Night, November 27,1929 69
Steam Fire Engine No. 1, 1910........................36
Straw Mansion, E.A., 1893 25
Temple Adath Yeshurin, 1984 86
Textile Field, Opening Day, 1913.....................43
Titt, Banquet for the Lord Mayor, October 10, 1931 72
Triple-Decker, 1970 82
Trolley Car Barns, circa 1920 55
The Unitarian Church, 1893 24
Urban Renewal in the Millyard, 1971...............83
Varick Advertising Sign, circa 1925.................66
World War I Memorial, 1928 68
Yantis House, Reverend A.S., circa 1921 57